THE ART OF IAN KENNEDY

THE ART OF

Ian Kennedy.

Chs Ian Kennedy

CONTENTS

FOREWORD
BY GORDON TAIT

AN APPRECIATION
BY PHILLIP VAUGHAN
6

SEVENTY YEARS OF SUBLIME ARTISTRY
BY JEREMY BRIGGS
8

IAN KENNEDY IN CONVERSATION
WITH CALUM LAIRD
14

1950s
20

1960s
32

1970s
50

1980s
84

1990s
118

2000 AND BEYOND!
130

ACKNOWLEDGMENTS
158

PAGE 1
From Ian's personal
collection. Illustration from the
late 40s "just for practise".
©Ian Kennedy

PREVIOUS SPREAD
Cover, STARBLAZER #206
'BATTLEWAGON' (1987).

OPPOSITE
Cover, RED DAGGER #7
'KILLER KANE' (1980).

THIS PAGE
Cover, COMMANDO #982
'THE COP WHO WENT TO WAR' (1975).

FOREWORD

I thought I knew quite a lot about Ian Kennedy's art, and then I started working on this book. What happened next should not have taken me by surprise, but that's the beauty of great comic art. It works so well you sometimes fail to recognise why it's working so well. I started to explore in more detail the techniques, dynamism, and sheer talent that Ian grafts onto every page. I'm not just a fan anymore. I'm a student learning about great comic art from one of the greatest comic artists. I hope you continue to discover something new in Ian's work every time you come to this book too.

I recall Ian's story of how he wanted to be a pilot in his younger days. He told me he "would have been a lousy pilot, anyway". Well, perhaps a cliché, but the airways' loss is the comic reader's gain.

Ian, let me thank you for flying us first class all the way. You are the pilot, in the cockpit, on those pages.

Gordon Tait
Heritage Comics Editor
DC Thomson Media (2019)

IAN KENNEDY – AN APPRECIATION

I first came across Ian Kennedy's work in *The New Eagle* circa 1982. The editorial in #19 told the readers that there was a new artist on 'Dan Dare' from Dundee. Being from Dundee as well, this blew my mind – and so did the art.

I began to notice Ian's distinctive style in DC Thomson's publications, uncredited but instantly recognisable. *Warlord* covers, *Starblazer* covers, the odd interior sequential strip and most famously of all, on *Commando* covers. I began to seek out comics that featured Ian's work. Science fiction comics, war comics, football comics and girls' comics; was there nothing this artist couldn't turn his hand to?

I even taught myself how to draw by copying Ian's work! Week after week, this amazing artwork appeared through my letterbox, and I could not believe it was being created somewhere in the city I lived in. I fantasised about visiting Ian's studio and seeing him at work. Truly inspirational stuff!

I realised a dream when he agreed to do a class for me on the undergraduate comics module which I run, and he has been a visiting lecturer at the University of Dundee for the last eight years, inspiring a new generation of comics creators...

It is safe to say that Ian truly is a comics legend. His influence on a generation of comics fans and creators cannot be understated. This unparalleled collection of his art is long overdue.

Phillip Vaughan
Senior Lecturer
Comics & Graphic Novels
University of Dundee

WARLORD
SUMMER SPECIAL

IAN KENNEDY

PAGE 6
Detail from cover, RED DAGGER #20
'THE BLACK SAPPER' (1982).

PAGE 7
Cover, WARLORD SUMMER SPECIAL (1976).

PAGES 8-11
Detail from interior pages,
WARLORD ANNUAL 'SNIPER' (1982).

Ian Kennedy's artistic career began as a staff artist at the Scottish periodical publisher DC Thomson and Co. Ltd. in Dundee in 1949 and, despite going freelance in 1954 and "retiring" in 1996, he has continued his association with the company to the present day. His art style, be it for black-and-white comic strips or for full colour painted covers, is both photo-realistic and dynamic while his page composition is dramatic.

Although he has covered many different types of stories since his early days, both for DC Thomson and for others, in the 1950s his comic strip art tended to be for adventure style stories and westerns. By the 1960s, he had moved into working on the combat picture libraries with black-and-white strips and fully painted colour covers, while, by the 1970s, his strip work tended to take second place to his full colour covers which adorned annuals, summer specials and picture libraries for girls as well as boys. The worldwide success of *Star Wars* in the late 1970s led to his involvement in science fiction strips and covers in the 1980s while, as the British comics industry contracted at the end of that decade, in the early 1990s he returned to mainly colour

cover work before taking retirement save for a semi-regular slot on the covers of DC Thomson's *Commando* comics.

Charles Ian Kennedy was born in Dundee in 1932 and while growing up he was fascinated by the military aircraft flying from the nearby Royal Air Force and Fleet Air Arm bases, a fascination that stood him in good stead for his many aviation and combat illustrations to come. Too young to join the armed forces during World War II, and medically exempt from National Service afterwards, he joined Dundee's DC Thomson publishing empire in 1949. He has since come a long way from his first job of colouring in the black squares of their crossword puzzles to becoming their pre-eminent cover artist for weeklies, picture libraries, summer specials and annuals. However, it was in the text dominated DC Thomson story papers that his illustration work first came to prominence.

He provided text illustrations for 'It's Wickets That Count' in *Rover* beginning in 1954 and, despite becoming freelance from DC Thomson in the same year, he would continue to provide text story and feature

illustrations for the title during the 1950s. Although he did the *Adventure* comic strip 'Red Skull Branson' in 1955 and the cover strip 'Commando Jim' in 1960, it was mainly illustrations for text stories as diverse as 'Death Stalks On Silent Moccasins', 'Big Jack's Rag-Tag Railway' and 'Kubal The Great' that he provided for the title in the late 1950s. *Hotspur,* also kept him busy, from illustrations in 'The Rocket's Red Glare' in 1958 to 'The Soap Box Special' in the following year. This last tale continued over from the story paper version of *Hotspur* to the picture strip version when the comic changed style in October 1959, and he continued his work for the revamped title (mainly with text illustrations) before starting a run of comic strips beginning with 1962's science fiction tale 'The Spy in the Sputnik' and cricket strips 'The Blind Bowler' and 'Chained To His Bat' in the following two years.

Girls' titles were not left out with 'Kay Hamilton Show Jumper' in *Bunty* in 1959, and his art was in the 1958 and 1959 *Rover* annuals, which included a comic strip featuring WWII pilot Matt Braddock VC. As a freelancer, he was also able to work at the same time for a variety of other British comics'

publishers on titles including *Sun, Knockout, Thriller Picture Library, Cowboy Comics* and *Express Weekly*. Whilst DC Thomson at this time did not allow artists' signatures to be printed, he would often sign as "Chas Ian Kennedy" for other publishers, an affectation he has long since left behind, and he even managed an unusual printed credit in *Eagle Annual Number 8* as "Charles I Kennedy".

The 1960s continued his work for *Hotspur*, as well as returning to *Rover* with a long run of covers and feature articles covering subjects as diverse as The Grand National horse race and the Battle of the River Plate. Returning to girls' comics, he produced more work for *Bunty* in the early 1960s with such titles as 'Girls Of Pony Patrol' and 'Soldier Sally' in 1962 and 1963, before beginning a long run of work for the *Judy* annual. Unlike the boys' annuals of the same period, the DC Thomson girls' annuals of the 1960s and early 1970s were sumptuous affairs with full colour dust wrappers, internal colour photographs and many fully painted strips, whilst boys' annuals such as *Hotspur, Victor* and later *Warlord* had to make do with black-and-white photos, single colour tinted strips and

no dust wrappers. The 'Growing Up' strips were a fairly regular feature of the *Judy* annuals in the 1960s, which gave a potted life-history of famous names, and in the 1967 *Judy* annual he took on the life of prima ballerina Dame Margot Fonteyne. While normally thought of as a humour comic, he painted adventure stories for *The Topper* annual featuring 'Barlow's Boneshaker' car in 1967 and 'The Sky Shark' flying submarine in the following years.

By 1970, the *Judy* annual stories included 'Emergency Emma' who was trained to deal with all eventualities in her department store. His art is in virtually every 1970s *Judy* annual, from fully painted strips to covers, but his work wasn't just in the girls' annuals as annual art would become a regular part of his work during the 1970s. While he produced covers, features and strips for IPC titles like *Valiant, Scorcher* and *Hurricane,* for DC Thomson he did covers for the *Victor* annual, covers and strips for the *Hotspur* annual, and painted features for the *Sparky* annual, while 1977 began his long association with the *Warlord* annual which would last through the 1980s and on to the final 1991 book.

Warlord began as a weekly in September 1974 and his art first appeared in issue 5 with a feature on the history of the tank. This would begin a long run of features and covers for the title until its final issues in 1986. His art would also feature in virtually every *Warlord* summer special, either producing covers, centrespreads, features or fully painted strips for such popular characters as Royal Marine 'Union Jack Jackson' or pilots 'Killer Kane' and 'Cassidy', while he painted 'Code-name Warlord' himself in 1976's unique Peter Flint Special. Indeed because of the lower print quality of the boys' annuals, the summer special strips were the only times these *Warlord* characters appeared in full colour. While he also produced six strips for the *Warlord* annuals, his strip work in the weekly title was limited to two runs of 'The Tankies' in 1978 and a single run on 'Blitzkrieg Bomber' in 1981. As well as the *Warlord* summer specials, he provided covers for a variety of other specials in the 1970s from three *Victor* summer specials beginning in 1972 plus the solitary *Bullet Sports Special* in 1977 and the 1978 *Bunty* and *Judy* summer specials.

Warlord would not be the only DC Thomson war title that he would be heavily involved with during the 1970s. During the 1960s he had produced full length black-and-white internal stories for *Air Ace Picture Library* published by Amalgamated Press, later renamed IPC, many of which would be reprinted in IPC's *War and Battle Picture Libraries*, but January 1970 saw him switch sides in these small combat comics with the appearance of his first painted cover for DC Thomson's *Commando* featuring Stukas dive bombing an Allied aircraft carrier in issue 453 'Seek And Strike'. It would be the start of a long and productive relationship with the title which continues to the present day, however, unlike with

the AP and IPC titles, he rarely did internal strips for *Commando*. Indeed despite having completed around forty internal picture library stories for the competition over the years, for *Commando* he has only done a total of five different internal stories and, inevitably, they were all aviation related. The first two appeared in 1974, issue 813 'Jack's Private War' and issue 832 'The Sand Devils' were both set during the Second World War. However his artistic ability to create painted covers was not lost on the *Commando*'s Editor, Chic Checkley, and by the end of 1970 he had eighteen published *Commando* covers to his credit, one quarter of all the covers published that year.

Remarkably all these picture library covers did not detract from his working on the various weekly comics in the same decade. For IPC, he would work on the remarkable variety of *Battle*, *2000 AD*, *Starlord*, *Tornado*, and *Valiant*, as well their factual titles *True War* and *Speed & Power*, whilst in 1976 for DC Thomson, he provided comic strip stories for *Bullet* with the giant robot story 'The Smasher' and a contemporary invasion of Britain story about the crew of a Scorpion tank in 'Frontline UK'. This story would be reprinted seven years later in *Buddy*, a comic which would also reprint his 1972 *Wizard* strip 'The Winged Warriors Of Flame Island'. *Wizard* had been a consistent source of work in the years before *Warlord* began, with comic strips such as 'Bradley's Bowmen', 'Tiger McTaggart', 'Typhoon Tennyson' and 'When The Green Mist Came', as well as various covers for these and others such as 'Cannonball Kelly' and 'Old Smokey'. 1979 saw his work in *The Crunch* with 'Morgan's Mob' where he was the first artist to illustrate the Han Solo styled character of *Starhawk*, who DC Thomson would use in various titles throughout the early 1980s.

Indeed the success of science fiction in the cinema was not lost on comics publishers and the 1980s saw him working on *Blake's 7 Monthly* for Marvel UK beginning in 1981 and a highly regarded run on 'Dan Dare' in *Eagle* beginning in 1982 which ran for almost three years. Even before *Blake's 7* he was involved with *Starblazer*, DC Thomson's science fiction picture library. His first cover for *Starblazer* was issue 10 'Terror Satellite' in August 1979, and, while he never drew any of the internal stories, his paintings were used as the covers of over ninety of the title's 281 issues. He produced *Starblazer*'s first wraparound cover in March 1986 with issue 168 'Timeslay' and the majority of his covers for the title come in the period after this. Indeed, from 'Timeslay' to issue 186 'Starhawk', published in December of the same year, only four *Starblazer* covers are by other artists.

Covers remained as major a part of his work during the 1980s as they did during the 1970s both for IPC with *Gary Lineker's Hot-Shot*, *Ring Raiders*, *Wildcat* and *Eagle* amongst others, as well as for DC Thomson. At the beginning of the 1980s, DC Thomson published two monthly reprint titles, *Red Dagger* and *Lucky Charm*, and he provided fully painted covers for many issues of both. For *Red Dagger* his covers ranged from the WWII military 'Braddock Of Bomber Command' and 'Tiger McTaggart', through to dogs and football in 'That Mascot Called Monty' to a giant octopus in 'Terror In The Tall Tower', whilst *Lucky Charm* had horses in 'Trudy Ten Legs', ballet in 'Sandra Of The Castle Ballet' and gymnastics in 'Little Miss Feather Feet'. He also did a long run of covers for *Warlord* in 1981 and 1982, returning again in 1985. His covers for annuals and summer specials continued during the decade with four annuals for *Hotspur*, six summer specials and seven annuals for

Victor, and a remarkable eight summer specials and nine annuals for *Warlord*. Despite all this, he still had the time to illustrate both covers and internal strips for the *Judy* annual as well.

In addition to *Commando* and *Starblazer*, DC Thomson produced a third boys' picture library beginning in 1986 which ran for 418 issues to 2003. *Football Picture Story Monthly* had a similar style to its two stable mates, so it was inevitable that he would provide covers and, whilst each cover had to feature a footballing subject, as early as issue 14 in December 1986 he was able to get an airliner onto the cover of 'Hi-jack' while issue 61 'Goals for Survival' in December 1988 had an Arab-Israeli style war scene.

As the 1980s came to an end, so too did the majority of the comic titles. Despite all the war, science fiction, and football work, he would return to the female titles in 1990 when DC Thomson's long-running *Bunty* moved from newsprint to higher quality paper, allowing for fully painted covers. *Bunty*'s best known strip was 'The Four Marys' and he produced many 'Four Marys' covers during this period including ones that covered their school trip to America. Painting the school friends as cheerleaders with pom-poms in *Bunty* must have been quite a change from drawing pom-pom anti-aircraft guns shooting at Axis planes for *Warlord*, *Victor* or *Commando*.

He rounded out the 1980s with the two *Commando* annuals, providing wraparound covers for both of the soft cover books as well as cover style internal front pages for each of the short comic strip stories contained within them. Indeed it was for *Commando* that he produced some of his last new comic strips. Having illustrated many internal stories for *Air Ace Picture Library* in the 1960s before becoming the foremost *Commando* cover artist, he had only previously illustrated two comic strips for *Commando* both published in early 1974. This changed when *Commando* issue 2967 was published in July 1996 for which he drew the comic strip and painted the wraparound cover for the Vietnam story 'Cougar Squadron'. This was followed in February 1997

with a Korean War story, issue 3024 'Fury Strike', about a Royal Navy pilot flying Fury fighters, and the trio was completed with 'Bombs On Target!' in issue 3072, a WWII story about the crew of an RAF Lancaster bomber. 'Bombs On Target!' was published in August 1997 just before his 65th birthday in September and it was to be his final new strip published in a British comic.

Today, Ian Kennedy still lives close to where he was born, all but retired save for his ongoing association with DC Thomson via *Commando* covers. There is a slogan above his work bench which reads "It doesn't have to be a bloody masterpiece." It doesn't have to be, yet for a remarkable seventy years it invariably was, and still continues to be to this day.

Jeremy Briggs has been a member of the team on the downthetubes.net comics website since 2007, contributing news, reviews, interviews and historical articles on British comics and their creators. He has written features for Titan's 'Johnny Red' and 'Dan Dare' reprint books as well as having contributed to the Ilex books *500 Essential Graphic Novels* and the Eagle Award nominated *War Comics: A Graphic History*. His articles on *Eagle* and its artists have appeared in *Illustrators*, *Eagle Times* and *Spaceship Away*, and he has lectured to the Eagle Society on the history of DC Thomson's comics. He has been a fan of Ian Kennedy's artwork since he first saw the cover of the 1976 *Warlord* Summer Special in his local newsagent.

IAN KENNEDY

The following excerpts are from a conversation which was recorded in January 2019. Ian Kennedy and Calum Laird met at the Dundee offices of DC Thomson's Archive Department, where they were surrounded by only a small selection of the vast body of Ian's original artwork stored there.

PREVIOUS SPREAD
Cover, COMMANDO #2967
'COUGAR SQUADRON' (1996).

PAGES 14-15
Detail from interior pages, COMMANDO #2967
'COUGAR SQUADRON' (1996).

PAGES 16-17
Detail from interior pages, COMMANDO #3024
'FURY STRIKE' (1997).

PAGES 18-19
Detail from interior pages, COMMANDO #3072
'BOMBS ON TARGET!' (1997).

CL: You've had 70 years in the business, Ian, but your drawing started well before 1949, didn't it?
IK: I always loved drawing. From my early years, Mum and Dad knew that to keep me quiet they just had to give me pencil and paper. As a teenager, once the evening meal was cleared away, the kitchen table was mine and I just doodled away.

CL: Your first job was with DC Thomson?
IK: Yes, I'd gotten a Scottish Higher in Art and had some informal coaching from one of DC Thomson's illustrators, Dave Ogilvie. That's when I learnt to use the dreaded dip pen and ink. When it was time to leave school, he must have "had a word", as I left school, had a fortnight's holiday, and went straight into the Art Department.

CL: What did they start you on?
IK: After being the tea boy for a few months, I started with a *Sunday Post* crossword, inking in the black squares and adding the numbers. That was my very first commercially published piece of illustration.

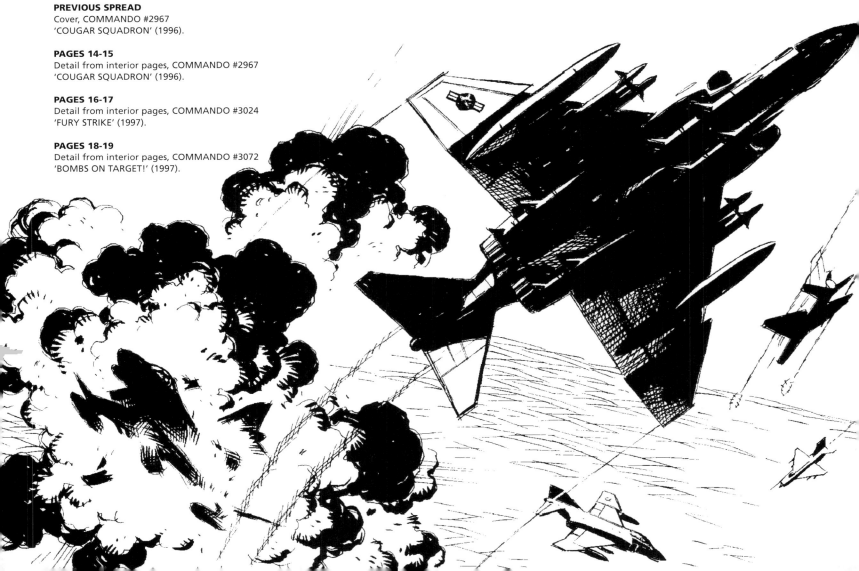

CL: I've noticed that you always pay tribute to the people in the studio at DC Thomson and the grounding you got from them.

IK: It was the best possible apprenticeship. Without it, I certainly would not have had the success I've had during my lifetime in art. For six months I was given used headings and illustrations to copy for practice. I cottoned on to the work of George Ramsbottom because I admired it so much. If I was working along the right lines, he would say, "That's a beezer". If I wasn't… wow, he didn't mince his words. That was where I learned to draw commercially, and developed a thick skin, because you're going to take criticism in this field.

CL: Eventually you did the story headers and the spot illustrations?

IK: Eventually, yes. The first illustrations were for the *Wizard* quizzes, it was a half page and the questions had wee sketches for each of the alternative answers. So I did that and eventually got on to header illustrations. And that was it for the next few years.

CL: You left the mighty DC Thomson in 1954.

IK: Well, at that time I was married with a young son and earning £7-10 shillings a week, and I felt I needed a bit more money. There was an artists' agent in Dundee called Bill McCail and after a bit of persuasion from one of my pals, fellow DCT artist Doug Phillips, I asked him to take some of my samples to London where he had connections. He came back with the news that I would have no problem earning £20 a week working for the publishers down there. They also said they could supply me with plenty of work. So I went freelance.

CL: In the circumstances it was the only thing to do!

IK: I have to make it plain that I never did make £20 a week, but I did double my salary.

CL: We have talked in the past about how you juggled your workload, particularly when your children were young. Were you always very disciplined?

IK: No, I was taught a sharp lesson that I learnt when I first went freelance. I was a keen golfer and thought I could balance days on the course or practice green with work. But then a note came in from one of Fleetway's directors saying, "What's this chap Kennedy up to? He's not keeping to the deadlines." After that, the job came first, not golf!

CL: Did you work to a very strict timetable?

IK: Well, I didn't have a strict timetable as such, but by instinct or experience I would know on seeing the script if I could do it in the time available. If I couldn't then I would say so. I remember one Editor telling me he always visualised me looking at my diary when discussing a deadline. The truth is it comes off the top of my head, I just know whether I am able to do a job. Not being a very fast worker, I built in a cushion of time to allow for things going wrong. 99 times out of 100 things went smoothly and it worked out fine.

CL: Your first freelance work was for Fleetway on *Knockout*. What work were you doing for it?

IK: 'Davy Crockett' was one character and if it wasn't him it would be 'Hopalong Cassidy'; it was all Western stuff, and that led to strip work.

CL: Now, I know that you dislike drawing horses, how did you manage?

IK: I don't know! When I looked at some of the stuff I did which contained horses I was quite surprised at how well they turned out. At DC Thomson, George Ramsbottom could draw beautiful horses so maybe something rubbed off when I was copying his drawings for practice in the early days.

CL: It amazes me that you say you don't like drawing horses because you draw them well.

IK: I probably traced them. Tracing paper is a very useful tool.

CL: You didn't do any strip work while you were in the DC Thomson studio, that started after you went freelance, didn't it?

IK: That's right, that development didn't start taking place until I had actually left so that would be after 1954. The strip story had already got going down south. The one that I remember most was 'Air Ace', just like our *Commando* of today. I didn't do any strip work before I went freelance. My first strip work for DC Thomson was probably for *Adventure*.

CL: Looking at your 'Commando Jim' cover pages from 1959 -1960, you were still working as a freelance artist then?

IK: Oh, yes, I remember those. I delivered them straight to the office. They would get pencil roughs, check them, and ask for adjustments if needed. Then I'd hand in the line work at the next visit.

CL: Did you have any input on the colour?

IK: No, they did it all. If I remember correctly, two floors down from the editorial office there was a little department where they did most of the coloured editions.

CL: Presumably you got a script that said which panels they wanted on the front cover but beyond that you'd have full control of the layout of the pages?

IK: Even then I had a fair idea of what the layouts were going to be. To be honest, though, there was still a fair amount of movement in all directions as far as layouts were concerned. Most of us were still finding our way and you have got to remember I was still a young apprentice.

CL: Your *Adventure* pages have strict regular panels; your later *Warlord* ones have irregular panel shapes and layout. You've gone from composing each picture almost separately to composing an entire page.

IK: I was playing around with the shapes to make each page something to look at as a whole. As long as you maintained continuity it was pretty much no holds barred. Continuity must be maintained.

CL: I think audiences prefer less restrained layouts now than they did in the 1960s. It has taken time, hasn't it?

IK: I think that because we live in a much more visual world now it demands much more from us in a way of putting things like that together to get the desired impact.

CL: Did you ever see a printed page you'd drawn and think, "Why on earth did they put the balloons and panels there?"

IK: No. I suppose having finished one job I was immediately on to the next, so going back and looking one over critically to see whether or not the balloons have been put in the right place never occurred to me. I'd moved on.

CL: When we looked at your early *Adventure* pages, it was easy to tell it was your work from the figures. I can see trademarks that you still employ. You found your style really quickly, didn't you?

IK: Yes, I suppose the basics showed up fairly early. It's like handwriting, the signature of a 20-year-old is going to change by the time they are 60 or 70 but the basics are still there. If you take a range from the early days until now there will be quite a difference in lots of detail ways, though. I am very fortunate in that I am still having fun trying out new things.

CL: Everyone notices the amount of detail you put into things. If an aircraft has crash-landed you'll show all the broken bits, not just the plane. Is it a compulsion to put in that little bit extra?

IK: I tend to do that. I think, "There's an aeroplane that has actually crash-landed and has come to a halt." And I say to myself, "All the time it is going along the ground it is bound to be shedding bits and pieces." So that's why I show them.

CL: You could get away without that, you don't need to do it. No one would know.

IK: I'd know.

CL: The other thing you do is to put in just enough other detail to suggest to the viewer that there's even more. You've done what's needed to let the brain of the reader finish it off.

IK: That's it. When I was a teenager, Dave Ogilvie, showed me a small etching of the bridge at Avignon. It was only one thin pen line starting on one bank and going across to the other bank. When I admired how simply it was done, Dave said, "Yes, the best artists always know what to leave out." I related this story to Dave Gibbons and he said, "Ah, no, no you cannot get away with that, Ian, the folks want to see what you put in."

CL: Did your eye for detail help when you were drawing and painting spacecraft for *Starblazer*?

IK: It must have done. Someone was talking to me about the spacecraft I was devising and designing and said, "When I see one of your designs, I know it's going to work, there is no way it won't work." It's how my mind works, I suppose, and for a total non-mathematical and non-mechanical kind of person it's unbelievable.

CL: Using the *Reader's Digest Household Repair Manual* for some of the shapes paid off?

IK: Oh yes. A very useful book, that was.

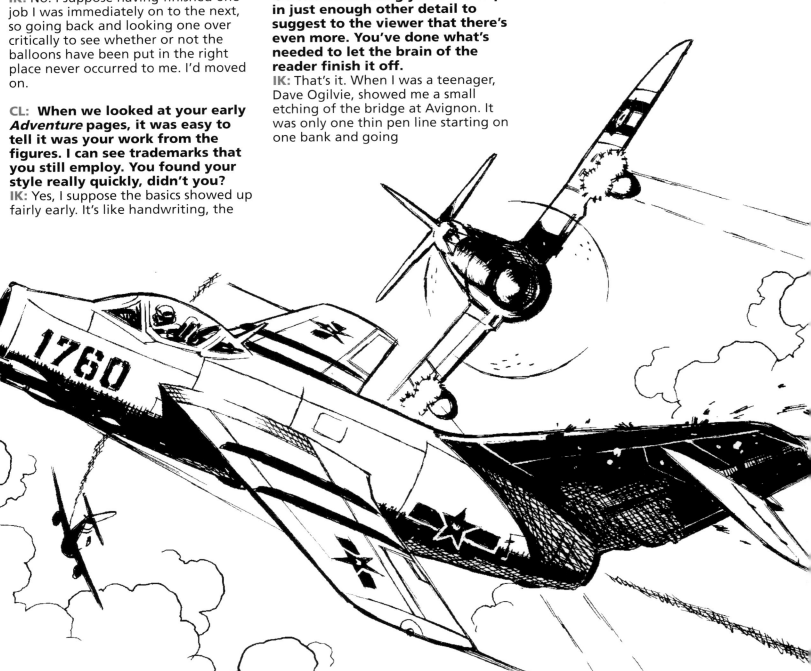

CL: Looking at your work, Ian, I think you're more mechanically inclined than you say.
IK: There are times when I wonder if I am an artist or a technical bloke. I sometimes wonder if a picture is getting too mechanical and technical. I always draw back then and let the art take over.

CL: If you hadn't been an illustrator I think you could have been a graphic designer because of your ability to balance the elements on a page.
IK: Yes, you are probably right. At school, as well as what we just called free hand drawing, part of the art course was Techie Drawing, where we learned how to draw simple plans. That tuition is part of my experience.

CL: In amongst the huge number of *Commando* covers you've done, there are a fair number with a single figure or object front and centre and a background that is very much a graphic design.
IK: Yes, I do have a very strong sense of design and I can't help it. I suppose that I bring that design sense into the aerial dogfights I love to paint. I have got a very strong colour sense that can cause problems at home when we're discussing a change in colour of something and I immediately think (and say), "That won't work."

CL: We've joked about this one ['Legend of the Longbow'] before, as the character looks like [the ex-head of DC Thomson's Art Department] Bill Stirton. You placed an RAF officer in front of a huge roundel. No other background.
IK: There is perhaps something instinctive there, but this is also where experience counts. It's a huge influence on being able to balance cover elements quite quickly. As you were saying, if you, or George or Ian in the past, presented me with a rough idea for a cover, nine times out of ten I could see that cover right away. You would notice right away that I had already dissected the idea. Then you would be able to tell me how you felt when I outlined my ideas for it more or less straight away.

CL: You are also quite methodical when it comes to covering the over paint at the edges of your illustrations.
IK: That's just something about me, I always feel I have to tidy it up.

CL: Even though you know it's not necessary, it's just your thing to tidy up?
IK: I started using masking tape on the cover edges. I tried putting the masking tape on, doing the job then taking it off, but the whole thing started to strip off! Panic stations! There was no way I was going to use that again.

CL: Turning to the tools of the trade, you said you started with a dip pen. I can see how that would be fine for line work but you would need to use a brush for filling in larger areas?
IK: I started with the dip pen but you'll find that as time went on, I didn't use it nearly as much. I began to use fine brushes quite a lot, so it was a combination of the two, with a broader brush for larger areas only. On most of my pages, you may be able to see the brush strokes.

CL: Some of the later black-and-white pages have a subtle grey wash in some areas, rather than a solid black.
IK: It was generally done just using the same black ink, just watered down. Again, it's brush work. This ['Chained To His Bat'] is me playing around with light and shade and contrast. I can remember one of the editorial staff

being a bit worried about the use of tones and blank space. I had to point out to him that white is a colour as well and that even if it is the white of your board, it's constantly used as, in effect, another colour. You can see how I used it in a lot of my inside pages.

CL: At what point did you start using fibre pens rather than the dip?

IK: It's difficult to put a date on it, maybe the start of the 1980s. When something like that comes on the market and I see it on a shelf in an art shop, experience tells me to buy one, take it home and doodle and see what I can do with it. Pretty soon you could get them in a tremendous variety of grades and gauges from very fine to quite broad, and with different profiles. There was a transitional phase from using the pen and ink to using fibre brushes. There may well have been times when I used both on the same job, because the size I wanted wasn't available in the new pens. I think most of my colour strip work since has been done using these pens. The one thing you have got to make sure of is that they are totally waterproof.

CL: I recall on one of the 'Great Warriors' covers we did in 2014 when you started to put on the colour you realised the pen work was running. It wasn't waterproof even though it was supposed to be!

IK: I'm afraid that some of the manufacturers tell you they are waterproof and they aren't because as soon as you put water on it that's it, you've got to blot it. That's when the acrylic colours come to your rescue because you can mix them up more thickly and cover the area without more smudging.

CL: When did you start using acrylic paints for your colour work?

IK: Oh, that's dead easy to answer. They came in just as I was starting on *Commando* covers, 1970/71.

CL: You'd done colour work before then, though?

IK: I really didn't start doing colour work until into the 1960s. Yes, I did colour work before then, colour strip work for the likes of the *Judy* Annual. They were done using line and coloured inks. Acrylics were much easier, much more forgiving to use than inks. When I started off I used them like oils with a sketch underneath and paint over the top. I did that for quite a few years. It was fine for covers but too slow for coloured strip work. So, I changed to doing a black-and-white drawing which I then coloured up like a children's paint book. You can do that with watered down acrylics, using them like watercolours, but thickening them up for a really punchy patch of colour.

CL: So, the foundation is a black-and-white drawing?

IK: That's right, the blacks all stay there and I paint over to colour it. From the drawing stage I could bring you a fully coloured page in just a couple of days. I could only really do that thanks to the acrylics.

CL: Is that the method you still use?

IK: More or less. I've been using these paints since 1970 and I'm still finding new ways of using them. But, yes, that is the technique I use today. The only difference is that now it's not so filled in, the black-and-white is a guideline that goes under the paint and you no longer see it.

CL: Are you still experimenting?

IK: Absolutely. Recently I was playing about and loaded my brush with black then rubbed it on a piece of blotting paper so it was almost dry and then dabbed it repeatedly to get a smudgy effect on the ground. I really do enjoy myself doing that and it gets a good effect, doesn't it?

CL: Yes, it works a treat and helps give even more movement within the cover. There's also a vibrancy about the acrylic colours that's very strong. I take it that appeals to you?

IK: With watercolours, if you don't quite hit the shade you want, and you try to paint over it, you lose the transparency, they go rather mucky and muddy. If you do that with acrylics you never lose the transparency, they become more vibrant which is marvellous for reproduction.

CL: How do you animate a static image without resorting to things like speed lines?
IK: Well, I like to do without speed lines if I can. I like blurring the background, or adding little spurts of earth flying to give movement instead. They give the sensation of movement by tricking the eye.

CL: As a commercial artist do you have to keep the reproduction of your art in mind?
IK: You have always got to remember that that was done for reproduction and reduction as well. So I would use the techniques that I developed for a painting for printing, whereas if it was something that was going to hang on the wall that would be a different matter altogether.

CL: A significant amount of your colour cover work has been for *Commando*. How did that come about?
IK: I'd done one or two colour annual covers and the then Editor of *Commando*, Chic Checkley, felt that he could use me for their covers and got in touch. After leaving to go freelance, I had been welcomed back into the fold quite quickly as far as DC Thomson was concerned, but I suppose that was when it was made absolutely final that I could do work for DC Thomson. All the Editors following Chic have used me as well so it must have been a good decision.

CL: What's more satisfying to you, the layout of a complete comic page or a finished cover?

IK: It doesn't really matter whether it is a cover or the outline of a cover, or a story page, so, irrespective of the nature of the job, if it is good enough to leave my drawing board, that's good enough for me. And I hope that it is good enough for the customer as well.

CL: You've illustrated everything from war strips to ballerinas, what subjects do you most enjoy?
IK: It's invidious to make a choice. Even if you were to pin me down and ask what's my absolute favourite, I don't know if I could tell you. I have always enjoyed the variety of the work I've been asked to do. Although I'm slowing up a wee bit, I'm still enjoying my art these days, but there are times when I look at my older stuff and I say, "I haven't improved much, have I? I wish I could paint as well as that guy there."

CL: You're still working for *Commando*?
IK: I do a cover for them every four or five weeks, mainly painting aeroplanes. As most readers of *Commando* have probably noticed, I delight in the juxtaposition of aircraft in dog-fights, playing around with angles, shapes, light and shade. Doing that is probably

me at my happiest. I've caused puzzlement in the *Commando* office over the years as to which way up the picture should be because of all the angles I like to use. Perhaps I should put an arrow pointing "this way up" to make absolutely sure they've got it right!

CL: You should. I did once print one of your covers 90 degrees out. It still looked spot on.
IK: It's all part of the fun! I maintain that, quite apart from the 5 years as an apprentice in the Art Department I was very lucky to have, I plied my trade during what I call the Golden Times. If a competent artist was out of work in those days then it must have been their own fault because there was so much work going. And it was such great fun.

CL: When you started with DC Thomson in 1949, if somebody had said that you would still be doing covers for them in 2019, would you have been sceptical?
IK: Yes, I would. It's been an interesting life and, thank goodness, still is. I have been so lucky to have been busy all these years, and I've never really given the future a thought, it has just come along.

Calum Laird joined DC Thomson in 1979 as a trainee Sub-Editor on *Jackie* magazine. In 1981, he transferred to *Commando* comics for the first of a number of tours of duty. In between these tours he worked on teenage girls' magazines (*Blue Jeans* and *Etcetera*), newspapers (*The Courier* and the *Evening Telegraph*), a motorcycle title (*Classic Motorcycling Legends*) and *The Dandy*. In 2007, he became the Editor of Commando following George Low's retirement. Over his career, Calum has been privileged to work with many of the talents who have made significant contributions to British comics, like Ian Kennedy. Calum retired from active duty with DC Thomson in 2015 to pursue an academic career studying… comics.

THE WIZARD

Cover, THE WIZARD #1350 (1951).
The pages presented here are from Ian's
personal collection. An example of the
printing process at the time, saved and
gifted to Ian by a colleague at the
DC Thomson art studio.

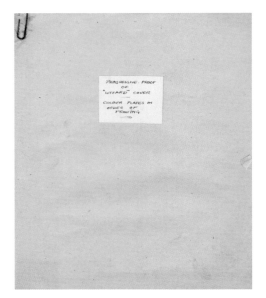
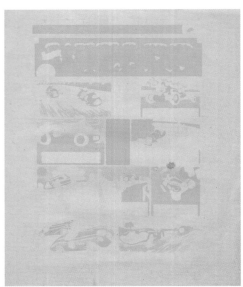

EVERY TUESDAY

THE WIZARD

Nº 1350
DEC. 29ᵀᴴ 1951
PRICE 3ᴰ

Two mighty midgets. Small car racing, begun in this country only a few years back, has become a firm favourite with drivers and fans. The king of these small cars is the Cooper (No. 11), which has an impressive list of victories behind it. No. 6, the J. P. (James Potts), is the only racing car built in Scotland. These small cars, with their engines in the rear, can lap tightly-cornered tracks at 70 m.p.h.

A challenge to the Cooper's supremacy in small car racing is the Kieft. This car, specially designed and built for the 1951 season, was driven to victory in its first race by Mr Stirling Moss.

Low, purposeful, with every line suggesting speed, the B.R.M. is Britain's challenge to the Continental racing cars for supremacy in Grand Prix racing. Not yet fully developed, the B.R.M. is capable of 200 m.p.h. on the straight.

These 15 fliers are some of the world's fastest racing cars. What of the men who handle them? It's been said that a top-notch racing driver is born then made. If you want to read the true-to-life story of the making of such a driver, if you want thrill piled on thrill, read inside—

"GREEN LIGHTNING"

No. 11, the B-type E.R.A. (English Racing Automobiles), another great British car, was a consistent winner in races before the war. Though out-of-date compared with more modern racing cars, this type of E.R.A. still manages to hold its own. The Talbot Lago (No. 40), a French car, is one of the fastest to come from the Continent.

Since the war most of the Grand Prix races have been won by one or other of these great Italian cars, No. 13, the Alfa Romeo, the Maserati (No. 1), and the Ferrari (No. 3). Here are the three in a tense speed duel.

M.G. (Morris Garage). This famous car has been winning races for years, and in its class is unsurpassed for speed and reliability. It is still a winner in sports car races and rallies.

Two of Britain's top racing sports cars are the Allard (No. 23) and the Jaguar (No. 20). Drivers of these cars have had many thrilling successes, including production car races, time trials, hill climbs and road races.

Also high in the sports car class are the Frazer-Nash (No. 16) and the Healey Silverstone (No. 12), two British cars which have done well in the Le Mans 24-Hours' Race and the Mille Miglia, an Italian road race of almost a thousand miles.

SON OF THUNDERHOOF

556.

THE STORY OF A DARTMOOR PONY

STORY PAPERS

DC Thomson's early comics were story papers which had a title illustration to accompany the text.

MAIN PICTURE
Scraperboard Illustration, from Ian's personal collection (1950). This technique was seldom used as it was very time-consuming. Watching a colleague in the Art Department who was using the method, Ian decided it would lend itself to this subject, and he fancied "having a go". Publication unknown at the time of going to press.

TOP LEFT
Illustration, THE WIZARD 'SON OF THUNDERHOOF' (1952).

TOP RIGHT
Illustration, THE HOTSPUR 'I WAS A SECRET FLYER' (1950s).

I WAS A SECRET FLYER

By Nick Waring R.A.F.

3/0S × 3¾" Deep   HOTSPUR

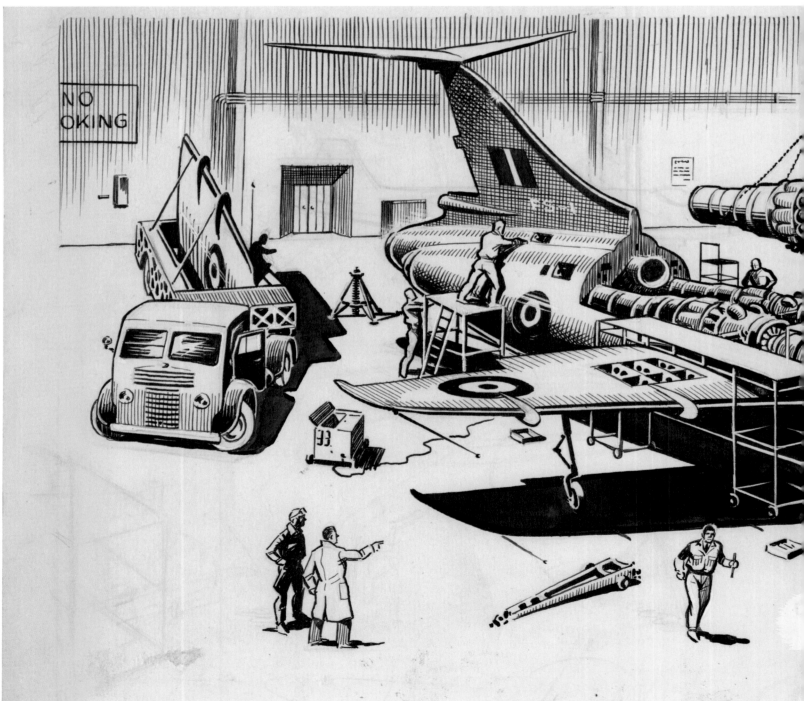

Illustrations, THE WIZARD 'TEST PILOT Z' (1950s).

TEST PILOT Z

BRITAIN INVADED!

Illustration, ADVENTURE 'BRITAIN INVADED!' (1952).

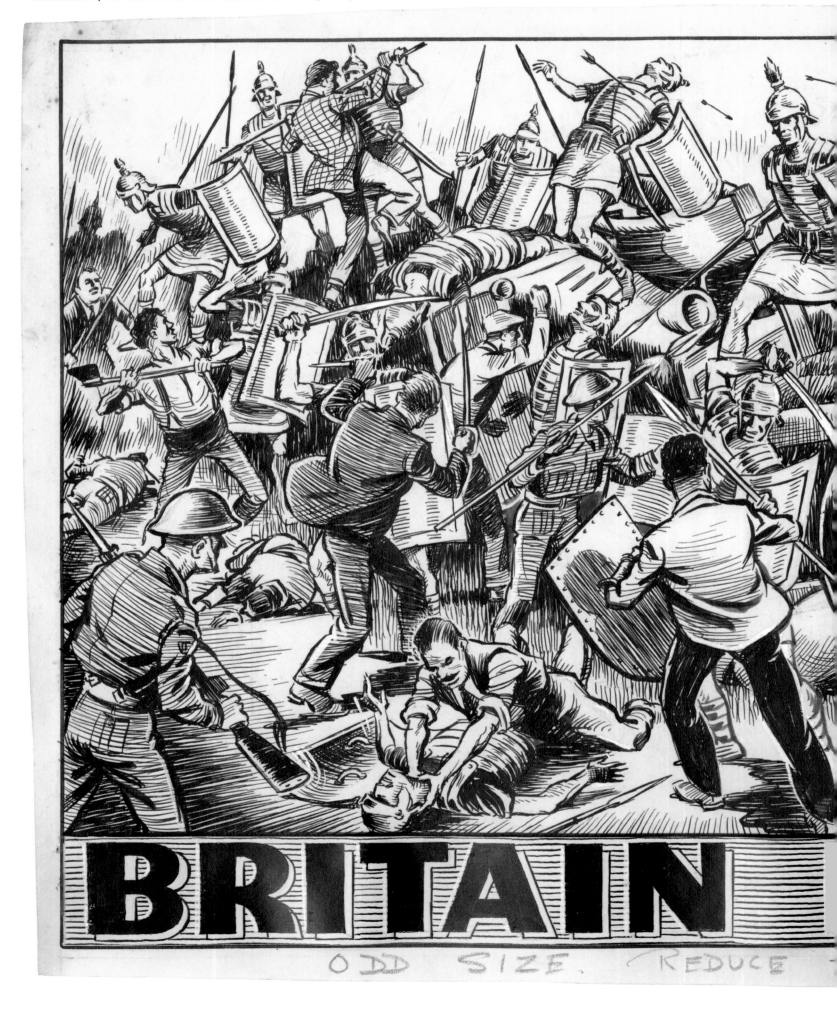

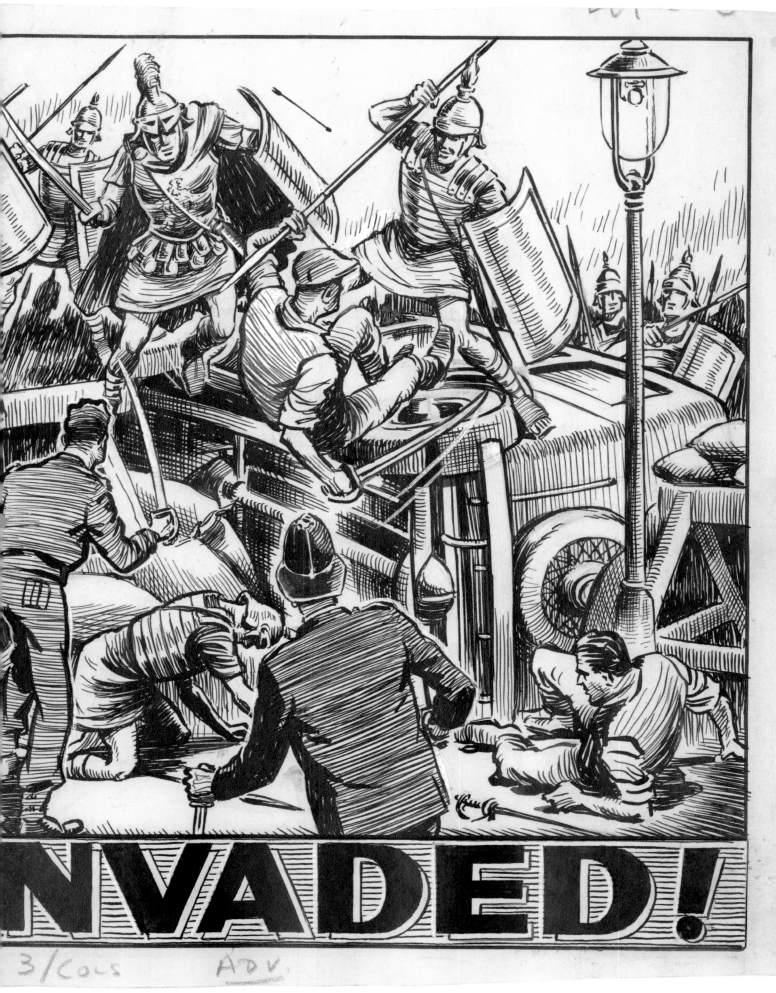

RED SKULL BRANSON

'Red Skull Branson' was one of Ian's first projects when he started freelancing for DC Thomson in the mid 1950s. The scripts were immaculately detailed and handwritten by Adventure's Chief Sub-Editor, Ralph Duncan.

The stories were told in a sequence of illustrations with the text placed below. No speech balloons or panels were used.

"Branson has his hands on his hips and, grinning a little, he is staring thoughtfully at this motor."
[Instructions for panel 4, opposite].

THIS PAGE
Original script, ADVENTURE 'RED SKULL BRANSON' (1955).

OPPOSITE
Interior art, ADVENTURE 'RED SKULL BRANSON' (1955).

Remove inside from engine is indicated

WITH THE COMPLIMENTS OF RED SKULL BRANSON

POLICE 21

71 BT 1629

EXCELSIOR BRICK WORKS

STUDIES

Studies from photographs
(date unknown).

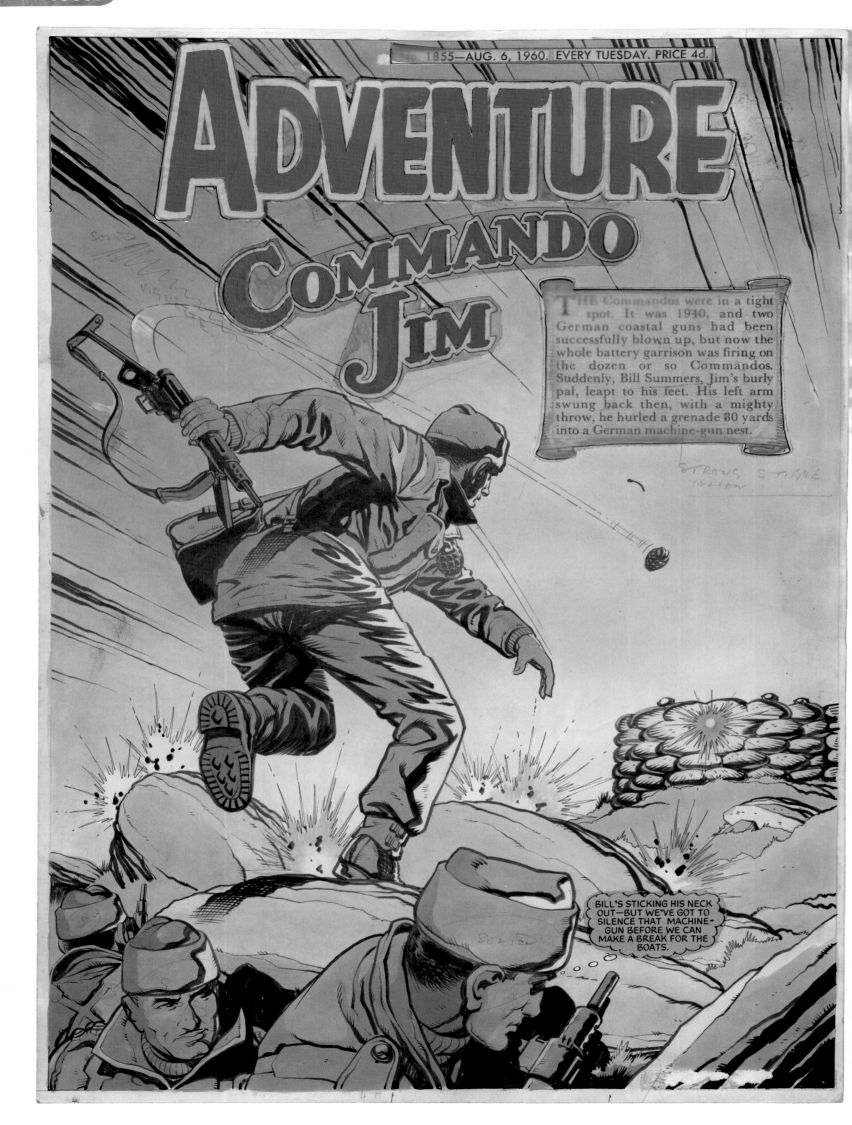

COMMANDO JIM

PAGES 32-35 ADVENTURE (1960).
Colour would be added to Ian's black-and-white line
work by the talented colour artists at DC Thomson.

SOLDIER SALLY

IN 1940, when Britain was at war with Germany, Sally Howard joined the Auxiliary Territorial Service, the woman's branch of the Army. She was posted to Buckdown Camp, where she was being trained as a height-finder attached to an anti-aircraft regiment of the Royal Artillery. After a week at Buckdown, Sally and the rest of her company fell in for Pay Parade.

As Sally was about to leave with her ten shillings pay—

In spite of her protests, Sally had to stump up, as she was told it was a usual charge.

Later in their barrack room the other girls grumbled about the unfair charge of sixpence from their wages.

Sally told her grievance to Corporal Bennett.

Suddenly, a loudspeaker blared an order for the girls to report to Sergeant Topham on the gun-site.

Once on the gun site, the girls had no more time to think of their grievance.

When the practice was over, Sergeant Topham told the girls the good news that they would be moved to a firing camp the next week. Sally was wildly excited at the thought of positioning the guns for actual firing at last.

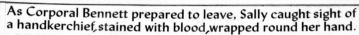
Back in the barrack room the girls received a shock.

LOOK AT THE WINDOW! IT'S BROKEN!

SO YOU CARRIED OUT YOUR LITTLE THREAT, HOWARD! WELL, YOU'LL BE ON A CHARGE FOR WILFUL DAMAGE. THERE ARE PLENTY OF WITNESSES WHO HEARD YOU SAY YOU'D LIKE TO PUT A BOOT THROUGH ONE OF THE WINDOWS TO GET YOUR MONEY'S WORTH.

BUT CORPORAL BENNETT—I DIDN'T DO IT!

As Corporal Bennett prepared to leave, Sally caught sight of a handkerchief, stained with blood, wrapped round her hand.

HOW DID YOU HURT YOUR HAND, CORPORAL?

OH, I ER—IT'S NOTHING TO DO WITH YOU, HOWARD!

LOOK, SALLY THERE ARE BLOODSTAINS BESIDE THIS WINDOW. CORPORAL BENNETT MUST HAVE BROKEN IT HERSELF FOR SPITE, AND CUT HER HAND IN THE PROCESS. SHE GOT TOLD OFF ABOUT LETTING YOU GO IN TO COLLECT YOUR PAY WITH YOUR CAP NOT STRAIGHT.

BUT SURELY EVEN OLD BENNETT WOULDN'T BE AS MEAN AS THAT.

Despite the injustice of the accusation, Sally was more worried in case she would be found guilty of the charge and be put in detention, thus missing being posted to the firing camp and having to stay behind with the next intake of recruits. Sally made up her mind to have the whole matter out with Corporal Bennett.

HERE COMES CORPORAL BENNETT. SHE'S GOT STICKING PLASTER ON HER HAND NOW.

MEDICAL OFFICER

CORPORAL BENNETT ABOUT THAT WINDOW...

IT'S ALL RIGHT, SALLY, THERE WON'T BE A CHARGE. IT WAS I WHO BROKE THAT WINDOW! IT WAS AN ACCIDENT.

I'M SORRY, SALLY. I PANICKED WHEN I BROKE THE WINDOW, TRYING TO OPEN IT. WITH THE SHOCK OF CUTTING MYSELF, I ACTED THE COMPLETE FOOL AND TRIED TO BLAME IT ON YOU. BUT YOU WON'T BE BOTHERED BY ME ANY MORE, SALLY. I'M GOING TO HAND IN MY STRIPES.

OH NO, YOU'RE NOT. YOU'RE COMING WITH ME TO HAVE A NICE CUPPA IN THE N.A.A.F.I.

LET'S JUST FORGET IT, SHALL WE? THE OTHERS' HEADS ARE SO FULL OF FIRING CAMP THAT THEY'LL HARDLY THINK OF IT AGAIN IF I SAY NOTHING.

On the following Tuesday, the girls prepared to leave Buckdown to go to the firing camp.

GOODBYE SALLY, AND THANK YOU— FOR EVERYTHING.

THE BLIND BOWLER

THE HOTSPUR (1963).

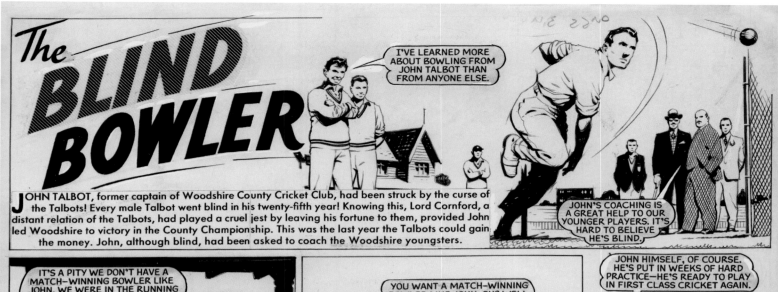

The BLIND BOWLER

JOHN TALBOT, former captain of Woodshire County Cricket Club, had been struck by the curse of the Talbots! Every male Talbot went blind in his twenty-fifth year! Knowing this, Lord Cornford, a distant relation of the Talbots, had played a cruel jest by leaving his fortune to them, provided John led Woodshire to victory in the County Championship. This was the last year the Talbots could gain the money. John, although blind, had been asked to coach the Woodshire youngsters.

> I'VE LEARNED MORE ABOUT BOWLING FROM JOHN TALBOT THAN FROM ANYONE ELSE.

> JOHN'S COACHING IS A GREAT HELP TO OUR YOUNGER PLAYERS. IT'S HARD TO BELIEVE HE'S BLIND.

> IT'S A PITY WE DON'T HAVE A MATCH–WINNING BOWLER LIKE JOHN. WE WERE IN THE RUNNING FOR THE COUNTY CHAMPIONSHIP AT THE START OF THE SEASON. NOW WE'RE LOSING ALL OU GAMES.

> YOU WANT A MATCH–WINNING BOWLER LIKE JOHN, EH? WELL I KNOW JUST THE PLAYER.

> WHAT? WHO IS HE, DOCTOR TALBOT?

> JOHN HIMSELF, OF COURSE. HE'S PUT IN WEEKS OF HARD PRACTICE—HE'S READY TO PLAY IN FIRST CLASS CRICKET AGAIN.

> THIS IS OUR LAST CHANCE TO INHERIT THE CORNFORD FORTUNE. I HOPE I CAN CONVINCE THE SELECTORS THAT A BLIND BOWLER CAN PLAY IN CHAMPIONSHIP CRICKET.

Despite being blind, Doctor Talbot, John's father, had become an eye specialist. He wanted the Cornford money to help in his research to cure blindness.

> THIS IS RIDICULOUS! I KNOW IT'S AMAZING THAT MY BLIND COUSIN JOHN CAN COACH, BUT PLAYING AGAIN IS A DIFFERENT MATTER.

> I AGREE WITH WEAKFORD— IT DOES SEEM RIDICULOUS.

Guy Weakford, John Talbot's cousin, was now captain of Woodshire. He alone knew that if Woodshire failed to win the championship, the Cornford fortune went to him. So Weakford was out to see that Woodshire didn't win the Championship!

> I'VE KNOWN DOCTOR TALBOT FOR MANY YEARS, HE WON'T HAVE MADE THIS DECISION LIGHTLY. I'VE DECIDED, AS CLUB CHAIRMAN, TO GIVE JOHN A TRIAL, IN A MATCH TO BE PLAYED BEHIND LOCKED DOORS.

> THE TRIAL WILL BE A FARCE. A BLIND BOWLER—I'VE NOTHING TO FEAR!

Two days later, at the trial, John prepared to bowl against Colin Taylor, the 1st XI's best batsman.

> HERE GOES! NOW I'LL FIND OUT IF ALL MY TRAINING HAS BEEN WORTH WHILE.

> THE WICKET KEEPER IS CLAPPING AS I ASKED HIM. THE SOUND WILL GUIDE ME—I HOPE!

BARLOW'S BONESHAKER

THE TOPPER ANNUAL (1967).
The first examples of full colour, sequential art, appear in print.

Mike and his Dad pressed on, just as fast as the old Bone-shaker could travel. Near civilisation now, they began to pass traffic on the road—and quite a lot of it passed THEM! Then at last they saw the outskirts of Johannesburg. They still had their lead—

—but not for long! Half a minute later, with a roar, the rival car streaked by!

It seemed as if the Boneshaker had been pipped at the post—until Jeff Barlow pressed a button on the dashboard. Suddenly flame and smoke began to belch from the back of the tough old car.

Rocket motors on! Hold tight, Mike!

THE SKY SHARK

THE TOPPER ANNUAL (1968).
The affect and influence of the decades' children's
television shows are apparent. Ian was, as ever,
absorbing all around him to attain the required
end results…with much success!

JUDY FOR GIRLS

DEEP SEA DEBBIE (1968). JENNY APPLESEED (1971).
The very earliest examples of Ian's painted colour work,
despite the publication dates.

Jenny Appleseed

JENNY was the granddaughter of Johnny Appleseed, a remarkable man who had devoted his life to raising apple trees and planting orchards in the newly-settled lands of Western America. Jenny had inherited both his skill and his miraculous powers over wild creatures. Now, in his old age, Johnny stayed at home raising the seedling trees, while Jenny, accompanied by Shining Grass, an Indian girl, made the long, hard journeys to plant new orchards and tend the growing ones.

THE APPLES WILL SOON BE RIPE, BUT THERE ARE NO SETTLERS TO EAT THEM.

ONE DAY THERE WILL BE A SETTLEMENT HERE, OR MY GRANDFATHER WOULD NOT HAVE PLANTED THE TREES.

SMOKE SIGNALS OF MY PEOPLE! THE SIGNALS SPEAK OF A RAID AGAINST THE WHITE MEN!

IT COULD BE THE SETTLEMENT AT CARIBOU REACH! WE MUST GO THERE!

SEEK AND STRIKE

Cover, COMMANDO #453 'SEEK AND STRIKE' (1970).
Ian's first cover for the publication to which he
would become inextricably linked.

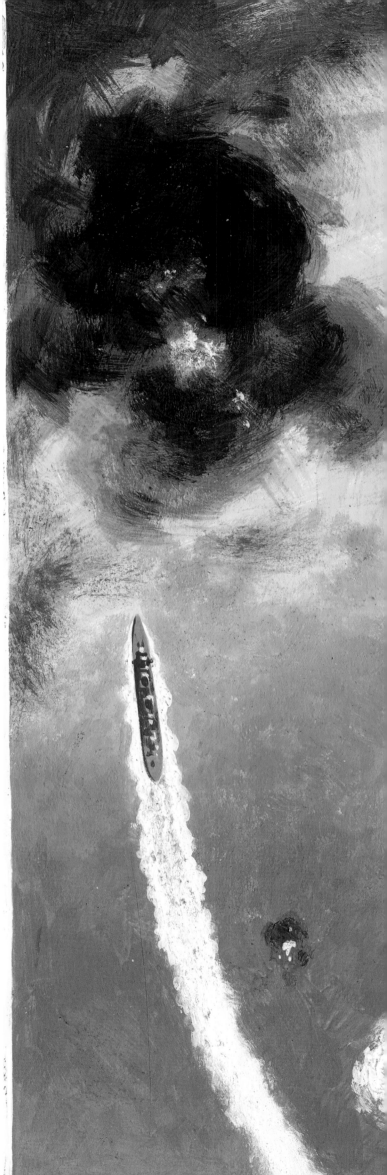

THE SKY SHARK

THE TOPPER ANNUAL (1971).
Telltale signs of when the artwork was originally created are seen in the detail. The number plate on the police vehicle indicates the year Ian actually painted the page.

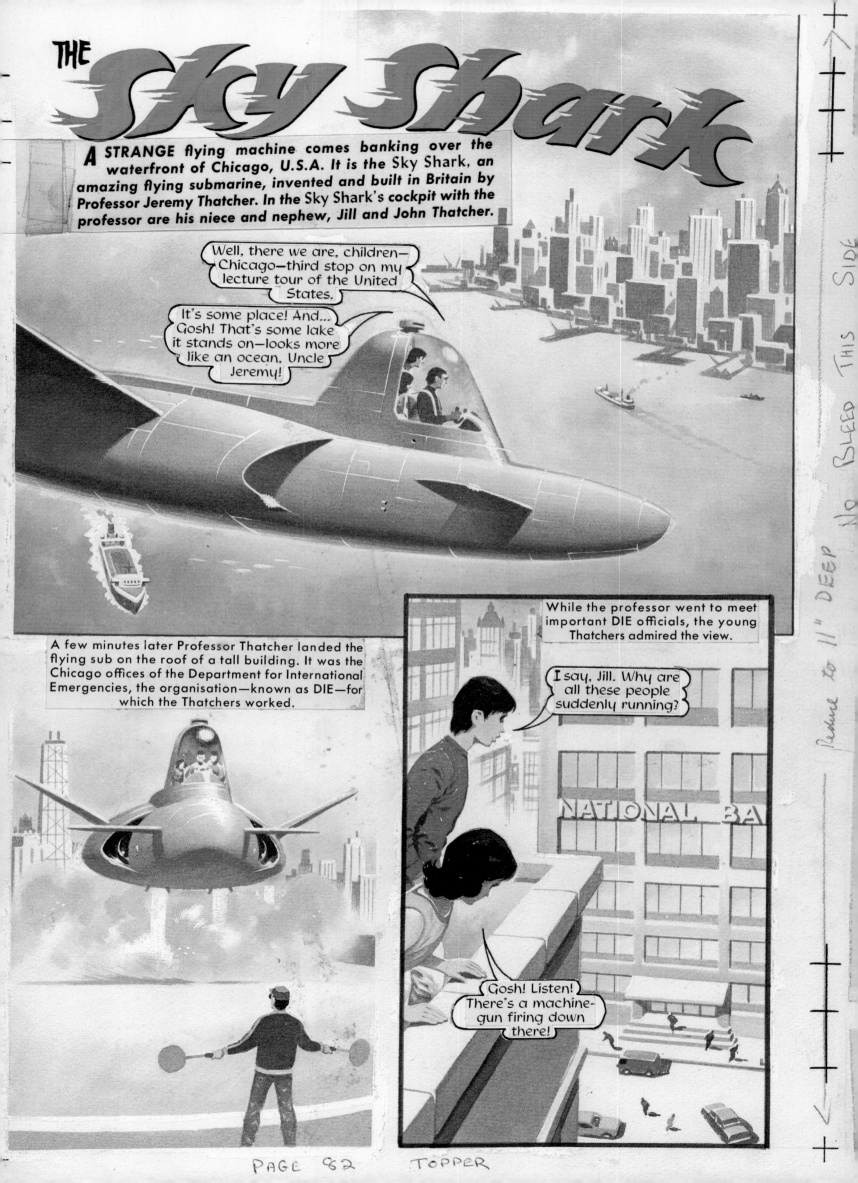

THE Sky Shark

A STRANGE flying machine comes banking over the waterfront of Chicago, U.S.A. It is the Sky Shark, an amazing flying submarine, invented and built in Britain by Professor Jeremy Thatcher. In the Sky Shark's cockpit with the professor are his niece and nephew, Jill and John Thatcher.

Well, there we are, children—Chicago—third stop on my lecture tour of the United States.

It's some place! And... Gosh! That's some lake it stands on—looks more like an ocean, Uncle Jeremy!

A few minutes later Professor Thatcher landed the flying sub on the roof of a tall building. It was the Chicago offices of the Department for International Emergencies, the organisation—known as DIE—for which the Thatchers worked.

While the professor went to meet important DIE officials, the young Thatchers admired the view.

I say, Jill. Why are all these people suddenly running?

Gosh! Listen! There's a machine-gun firing down there!

NATIONAL BA

JACK'S PRIVATE WAR

Cover, COMMANDO #813 'JACK'S PRIVATE WAR' (1974).

PREVIOUS SPREAD Cover,
COMMANDO #621 'TIGER IN THE TAIL' (1972).

PAGES 58-59 Detail from interior pages,
COMMANDO #813 'JACK'S PRIVATE WAR' (1974).

FULL FATHOM FIVE...

Cover, COMMANDO #893
'FULL FATHOM FIVE...' (1974).

SECRET OF THE SANDS

Cover, COMMANDO #945
'SECRET OF THE SANDS' (1975).

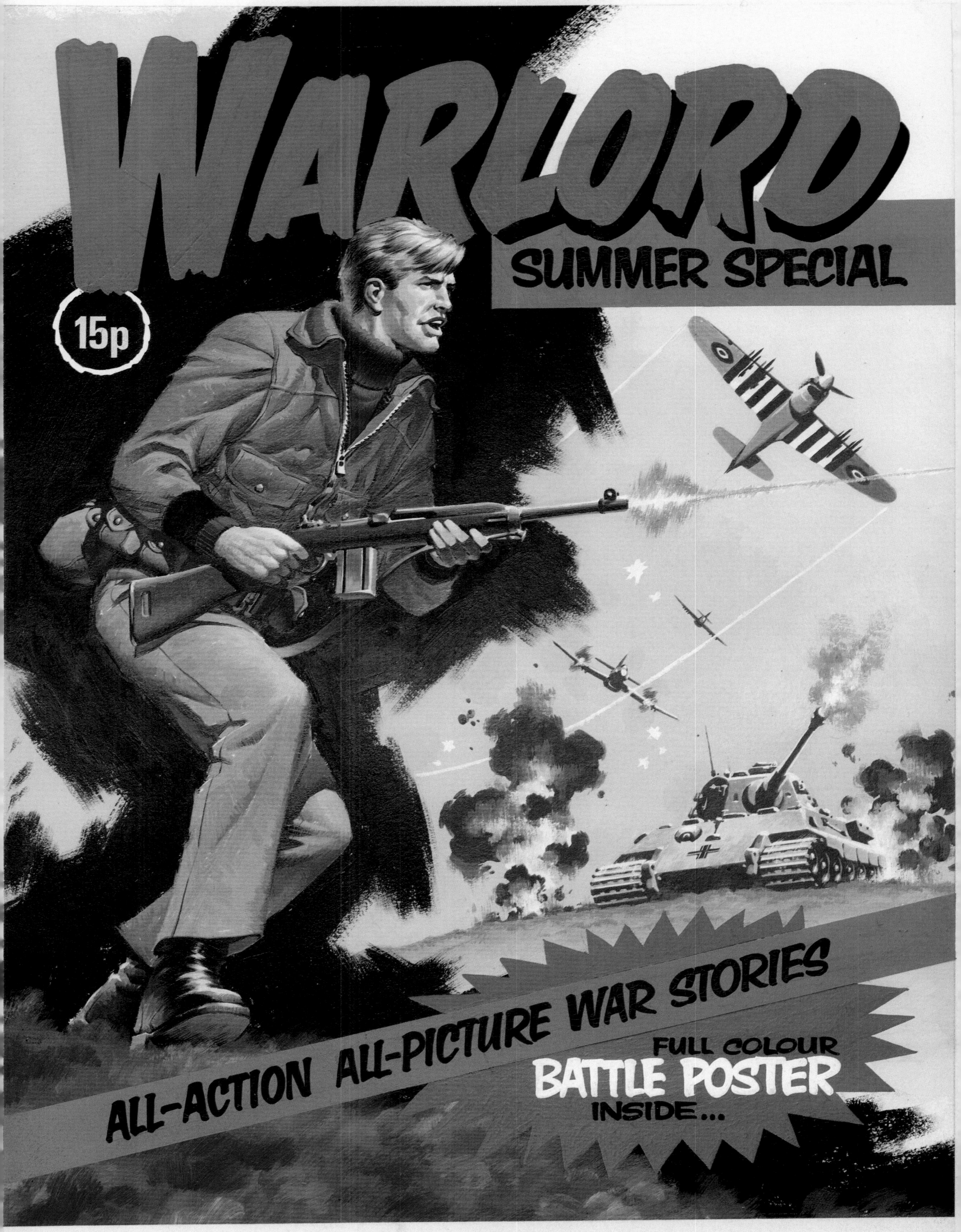
WARLORD
SUMMER SPECIAL
15p
ALL-ACTION ALL-PICTURE WAR STORIES
FULL COLOUR
BATTLE POSTER
INSIDE...

TANKBUSTERS

Interior pages, WARLORD SUMMER SPECIAL (1975).

PAGE 64 Cover, THE HOTSPUR ANNUAL 'THE BLACK SAPPER' (1975).

PAGE 65 Cover, WARLORD SUMMER SPECIAL (1975).

PETER FLINT ...

WARLORD
COMBAT
Pull-out poster

ONE MAN ARMY !

19 3/4" wide

AND **THIS** IS WHERE THE ACTION STARTS...

SMASHER

Interior pages, BULLET 'SMASHER' (1976).

PREVIOUS SPREAD Poster, WARLORD PETER FLINT SPECIAL (1976).

KILLER KANE

Interior pages, WARLORD SUMMER SPECIAL
'KILLER KANE' (1977).

"You know that when I draw these,
I am the pilot. That's me in the cockpit."
- Ian Kennedy (Dundee, 2019)

" WE'RE BOGGED DOWN! "
A hit! Try for the other now!
AAAGH!
We've copped one!
It's not serious! Keep firing!
Get going, you lot! We'll cover you from any more heavy stuff!
Hit everything you can see! The Jerries will take a while to recover from this little picnic.
Shortly, near where the convoy had been ambushed—
We've hit soft sand! We're bogged down!
Of all the luck! We'll try to tow you out!
Much obliged, Tankies! You proved more useful than I'd expected. We're off now! Put your foot down!
It's no use. We'll be stuck too if we don't watch out. You'll have to leave your tank and come with us!
T.3
WD.23.9.78

THE TANKIES

Interior pages, WARLORD 'THE TANKIES' (1978).

MORGAN'S MOB

Interior pages, CRUNCH 'MORGAN'S MOB' (1979).

UNION JACK JACKSON

Interior pages, WARLORD SUMMER SPECIAL 'UNION JACK JACKSON' (1979).

LEGEND OF THE LONGBOW

Cover, COMMANDO #1354
'LEGEND OF THE LONGBOW (1979).

STARBLAZER

The black-and-white, digest size science fiction comic series ran from 1979 until 1991 before being beamed up, up and away into DC Thomson's archives. Of its 281 issues, Ian contributed over 90 out-of-this-world full colour covers.

PREVIOUS SPREAD
PAGE 82
Cover, STARBLAZER #10
'TERROR SATELLITE' (1979).

PAGE 83
Cover, STARBLAZER #16
'THE SECRET OF SOMA' (1979).

THIS PAGE
Cover, STARBLAZER #51
'PRISONERS OF ZORR' (1981).

Cover, STARBLAZER #25
'GALACTIC SHOOTOUT' (1980).

Cover, STARBLAZER #85
'BEYOND THE BLACK HOLE' (1982).

Detail from cover, STARBLAZER #35
'LORD OF JARKNESS' (1980).

OPPOSITE
Cover, STARBLAZER #90
'RETURN OF THE PLANET TAMER' (1983).

LUCKY CHARM

DC Thomson's girls' comic was a magazine-size publication that collected and reprinted stories from their other girls' comics' back catalogue. The bi-monthly comic only had thirty issues and ran from 1979 to 1984. Some of Ian Kennedy's notable contributions to Lucky Charm's covers include 'Little Miss Feather Feet', 'Tug-o'-war for Flighty' and 'The Taming of Teresa'.

THIS PAGE
Cover, LUCKY CHARM #2
'SANDRA OF THE CASTLE BALLET' (1980).

Cover, LUCKY CHARM #18
'WONDER GIRL' (1982).

Cover, LUCKY CHARM #6
'TRUDY TEN-LEGS' (1980).

Detail from cover, LUCKY CHARM #16
'THE CHILDREN'S CHAMPION' (1982).

OPPOSITE
Cover, LUCKY CHARM #7
'ANGEL' (1980).

PAGE 88
Cover, LUCKY CHARM #14
'PAVEMENT BALLERINA' (1981).

PAGE 89
Cover, LUCKY CHARM #15
'TUG-O'-WAR
FOR FLIGHTY' (1981).

TARGET - CRETE!

Cover, COMMANDO #1478 'TARGET – CRETE!' (1981).

BLITZKRIEG BOMBER

Interior pages, WARLORD 'BLITZKRIEG BOMBER' (1981).

" LET'S BOMB THE TARGET!"

FRONTLINE UK

Interior pages,
BUDDY 'FRONTLINE UK'
(1983).

THE FIGHTING CONDOR

Interior pages,
WARLORD BOOK 'FIGHTING CONDOR'
(1983).

RED DAGGER

These magazine-size comics reprinted weekly character strips that had appeared in other publications, bringing them together – and on occasion expanding them – to create full-story single issues. Running from 1979 to 1984, there were 30 bi-monthly issues published alongside its sister title Lucky Charm.

THIS PAGE
Cover, RED DAGGER #13
'THE FROZEN MAN ON THE MOUNTAIN' (1981).

Cover, RED DAGGER #14
'MORGYN THE MIGHTY' (1981).

Cover, RED DAGGER #12
'BRADDOCK AND THE FLYING TIGERS' (1981).

Detail from cover, RED DAGGER #17
'THE SECRET OF BLACK ISLAND' (1982).

OPPOSITE
Cover, RED DAGGER #16
'TIGER McTAGGART' (1982).

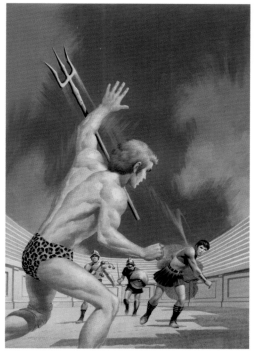

MATT BRADDOCK

Ian's superb rendering skills are abundant on the Red Dagger covers. Heroic characters are deftly executed as are the hardware, settings and even the fabrics.

THIS PAGE
Cover, RED DAGGER #29
'BRADDOCK OF BOMBER COMMAND' (1984).

BELOW
Cover art with the text overlay and the finished printed version.

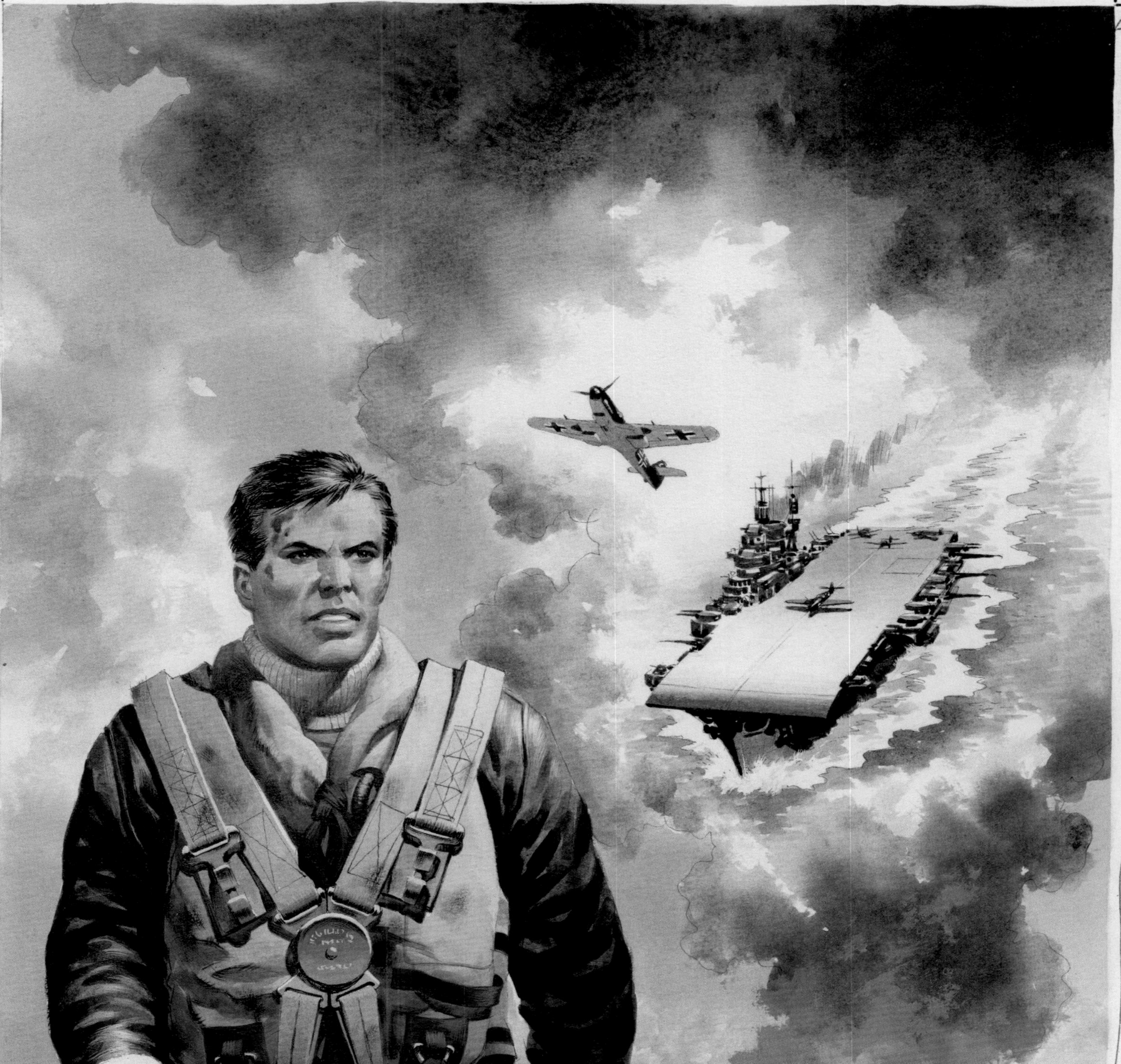

FOOTBALL PICTURE STORY MONTHLY

This popular, digest-size, black-and-white comic covered football stories and featured full colour covers, the very first being by Ian. It launched in 1986, spanning 418 issues before finally calling time in the early 2000s.

THIS PAGE
Cover, FOOTBALL PICTURE STORY MONTHLY #14 'HI-JACK' (1986).

OPPOSITE
Cover, FOOTBALL PICTURE STORY MONTHLY #9 'THE INVISIBLE MANAGER' (1986).

STARBLAZER

PREVIOUS SPREAD
Cover, STARBLAZER #186
'STARHAWK' (1987).

THIS PAGE
Detail from cover, STARBLAZER #101
'FORGOTTEN WORLD' (1983).

OPPOSITE
Cover, STARBLAZER #217
'THE PIRATES OF PENZ-ANZ' (1988).

PAGE 108
Cover, STARBLAZER #210
'DRAGON SLAYER' (1988).

PAGE 110
Cover, STARBLAZER #230
'A PLAGUE OF HORSEMEN' (1988).

PAGE 112
Cover, STARBLAZER #245
'ROGUE MANDROID' (1989).

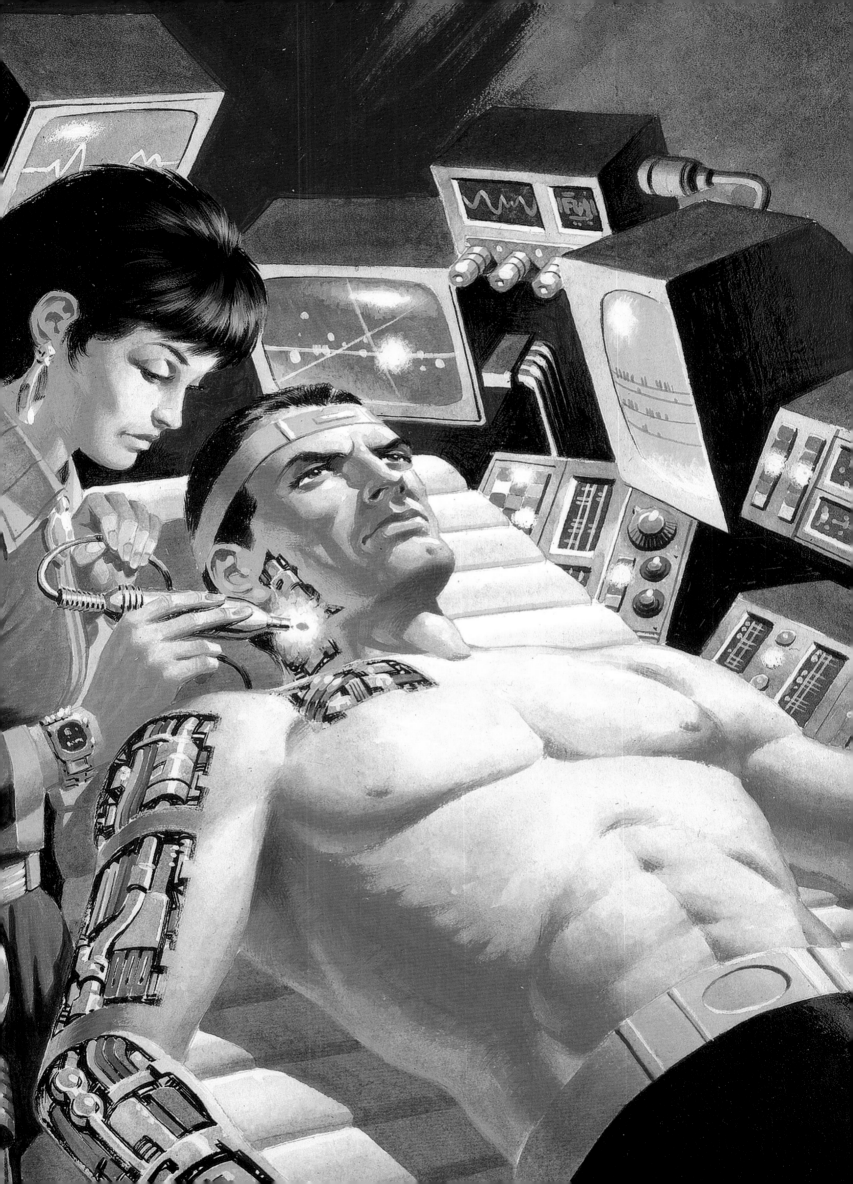

WARNER'S WAR

Cover, COMMANDO #2226 'WARNER'S WAR' (1988).

NEXT SPREAD
Cover, COMMANDO ANNUAL 1989 (1989).

"SQUADRON – SCRAMBLE!"

PREVIOUS SPREAD
Cover, COMMANDO ANNUAL 1990 (1990).

THIS PAGE
Cover, COMMANDO #2622
'"SQUADRON – SCRAMBLE!"' (1992).

NEXT SPREAD
Cover, STARBLAZER #266
'BADLANDS' (1990).

PAGE 124
Cover, STARBLAZER #267
'SKALD — THE SAGA CONTINUES…' (1990).

PAGE 126
Cover, COMMANDO #3009
'NIGHT OF RECKONING' (1996).

PAGE 128
Cover, COMMANDO #3024
'FURY STRIKE' (1997).

THE TRUTH ABOUT WILSON

Work on a dummy for a new comic began in 2002. The comic had the working title of Wizard. An intended mix of humour and action brought Ian to the project. He was tasked with illustrating an updated version of the character, Wilson. The Wonder Athlete first appeared in 1943's The Wizard.

RAMSEY'S RAIDERS

The rag-tag team of mavericks from the Special Raiding Force were an instant hit with Commando readers, the first two issues eventually being released in what became DC Thomson's first graphic novel. Ian's covers always show the team in the middle of the fight — something they're more than familiar with.

THIS PAGE
Cover, COMMANDO #3861
'THE RAIDERS RETURN!' (2005).

Cover, COMMANDO #3869
'RAMSEY'S ISLAND RAIDERS' (2005).

Cover, COMMANDO #3874
'RAIDERS' REVENGE' (2005).

Cover, COMMANDO #3877
'RAIDERS FROM THE SKY' (2006).

OPPOSITE
Cover, COMMANDO #3854
'RAMSEY'S RAIDERS' (2005).

BY SPECIAL REQUEST

OPPOSITE

Poster, NATIONAL ARMY MUSEUM 'DRAW YOUR WEAPONS' (2011).

To celebrate 50 years of its publication, Commando teamed up with The National Army Museum for an exhibit of original artwork. Ian Kennedy was asked to illustrate the poster for the event. The poster had a white background, with Kennedy's artwork cut out, whereas as you can see on the left, the original had a blue painted background.

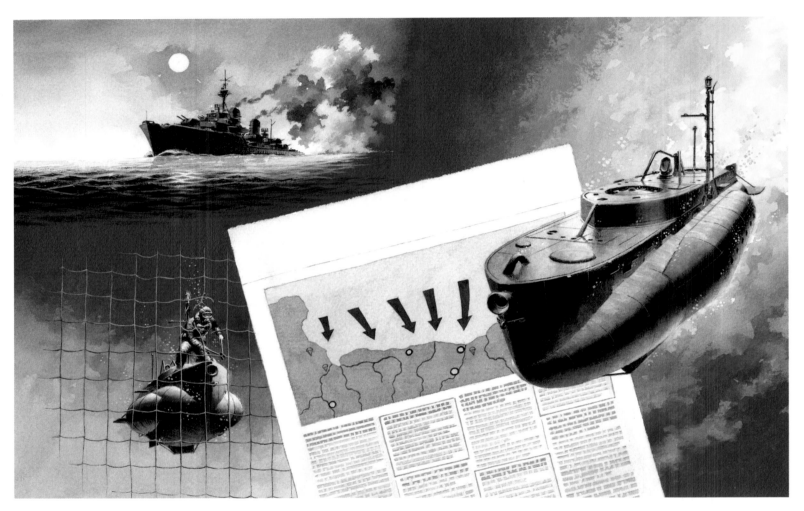

THIS PAGE

Cover, COMMANDO #2765
'TO LEAD THE WAY' (1994).

Originally printed in June 1994 to commemorate 50 years since Operation Gambit, in 2018 'To Lead The Way' was specially selected to be used as a place setting by the Royal Navy Submarine Service for their annual Operation Gambit dinner. The dinner was particularly special as it was attended by some of the individuals involved in the actual operation in 1944.

THE GHOST OF GOODWOOD

Specially commissioned as a supplement for the 2014 Goodwood Revival event, the short story complemented the celebration of the 70-year anniversary of Operation Overlord, and 75 years since Westhampnett Farm was turned into an RAF base.

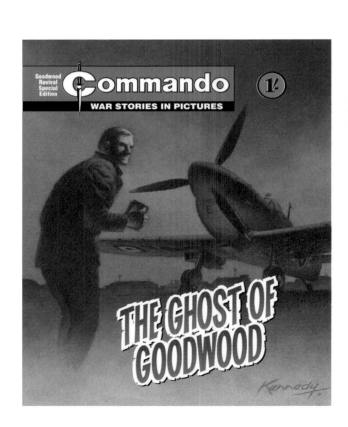

539 ASSAULT SQUADRON

Commissioned in 2016 for the 539 Assault Squadron, the amphibious arm of 3 Commando Brigade, Ian Kennedy's 'Fight the Raging Torrent!' depicts a scene from Exercise Raging Torrent.

THIS PAGE
Initial sketch outline and full cover (2016).

OPPOSITE
Unedited original artwork (2016).

THE GREAT WAR

Cover, COMMANDO #4671 'MIRACLE AT MONS' (2014).

THE GREAT WAR

THIS PAGE

Cover, COMMANDO #4679 'DEADLOCK AT THE MARNE' (2014).

Cover, COMMANDO #4687 'FIRST FIGHT FOR FLANDERS' (2014).

Cover, COMMANDO #4695 'ANZAC COVE' (2014).

OPPOSITE

Cover, COMMANDO #4703 'ATTACK IN ARTOIS' (2014).

THIS PAGE

Cover, COMMANDO #4739 'ATTACK IN ARABIA' (2014).

OPPOSITE

Cover, COMMANDO #4711 'FIRESTORM IN FLANDERS' (2014).

Cover,, COMMANDO #4723 'TO VIMY… TO VICTORY?' (2014).

Cover, COMMANDO #4731 'THE MINERS OF MESSINES' (2014).

THE GREAT WAR

THE GREAT WAR

THIS PAGE

Cover, COMMANDO #4747 'IN FLANDERS SKY…' (2014).

Cover, COMMANDO #4755 'CLASH AT CAMBRAI' (2014).

Cover, COMMANDO #4759 'ASSAULT IN THE ALPS' (2014).

OPPOSITE

Cover, COMMANDO #4767 'ARMISTICE!' (2014).

2014 saw the release of a year-long series of World War One stories in the pages of Commando. Ian provided all thirteen covers.

"I am very proud of this set. Something different happens during the work on this particular series and on anything related to The First World War. I lost an uncle to The Great War. It really felt like he was looking over me in the studio whilst I was transported into the scene. I was completely immersed in these. An experience not usually felt on the other covers."
Ian Kennedy (2019)

ISSUE 5000

A huge landmark, on the 9th of March, 2017, Commando released its 5000th issue, with a special red foil title and classic Ian Kennedy cover. The cover was so popular that is was a finalist in the fan vote for Best Cover at the PPA Scottish Magazine Awards 2017.

Cover,
COMMANDO #5000
'ZERO HOUR' (2017).

THE WEEKES' WAR

To commemorate 100 years since the signing of the Armistice of 11 November 1918, a special five-part series was released in November 2018. Ian designed the covers himself, taking inspiration from the series of covers he did four years previously to mark the beginning of The Great War.

THIS PAGE

CLOCKWISE FROM TOP LEFT

Cover, COMMANDO #5173 'DANNY'S WAR' (2018).

Cover, COMMANDO #5175 'MICHAEL'S WAR' (2018).

Cover, COMMANDO #5181 'TOMMY'S WAR' (2018).

Cover, COMMANDO #5177 'BILLY'S WAR' (2018).

OPPOSITE

Cover, COMMANDO #5179 'HARRIET'S WAR' (2018).

RAMSEY'S RAIDERS

Following the release of the graphic novel in 2018, the Raiders returned to the weekly Commando comic in January 2019. As you can see from the initial drafts and unedited cover artwork, the hiatus in the series had the Commando Team and artist guessing as Ian accidentally omitted Ramsey's signature eye patch.

THIS PAGE

First draft cover, COMMANDO #5197 'RAMSEY'S RAIDERS: RACE AGAINST TIME' (2018).

Second draft cover, COMMANDO #5197 'RAMSEY'S RAIDERS: RACE AGAINST TIME' (2018).

Cover, COMMANDO #5197 'RAMSEY'S RAIDERS: RACE AGAINST TIME' (2018).

OPPOSITE

Unedited cover, COMMANDO #5197 'RAMSEY'S RAIDERS: RACE AGAINST TIME' (2018).

THE QUARTERMASTER

Who better to introduce readers to each new issue of Commando than their very own Commando Quartermaster. Created as a spokesperson for the brand, the Quartermaster was commissioned in the autumn of 2018.

Kennedy

Kennedy

Kennedy.

COMMANDO VS ZOMBIES

Concept art for a proposed "special" issue of Commando.

Ian worked up the initial drawings and presented the colour rough to the team. He remarked that as he was working on the image, he couldn't help but think "whatever is next?"

Dedication

To my parents, who did all they could to encourage their son in his strange need to draw everything in sight.

Also, to David Ogilvie, an artist who was, eventually, instrumental in my being accepted as a trainee illustrator (tea boy) in the Art Department of publishers DC Thomson. The lasting influence of the five years I spent surrounded by so much professional experience cannot be overestimated!

Mention should also be made of the great number of "working friendships" made during my years in Children's Publications and Advertising etc., so many it would be wrong to single out anyone in particular. However, there is one individual who deserves recognition. Working all this time from home, frequently making an absolute nuisance of oneself, is not admittedly the best recipe for an idyllic relationship. With this in mind, the constant forbearance on the part of my wife, Gladys, is to be commended!

Acknowledgements

The Heritage Comics Team would like to give special thanks to Ian Kennedy,
Gladys Kennedy, Calum Laird, Jeremy Briggs, Phillip Vaughan, Paul Egan,
James Kirk, Iain McKenzie, Craig Graham, Sylwia Jackowska, the DC Thomson
Archive Department, and the DC Thomson Media Administration Department.

Cover
Compositing and digital art by Grant Wood.
Concept (above) and original illustrations by Ian Kennedy.

Photos of Ian Kennedy by Steven MacDougall at DC Thomson.

The Heritage Comics Team
Editorial
Georgia Battle, Kate McAuliffe, Michelle O'Donnell, Rhiannon Tate, Gordon Tait.
Designers
Leon Strachan, Grant Wood.

Editor-in-Chief
Alexandria Turner

Children's Publisher
Gareth Whelan

Head of Publishing
Maria T. Welch

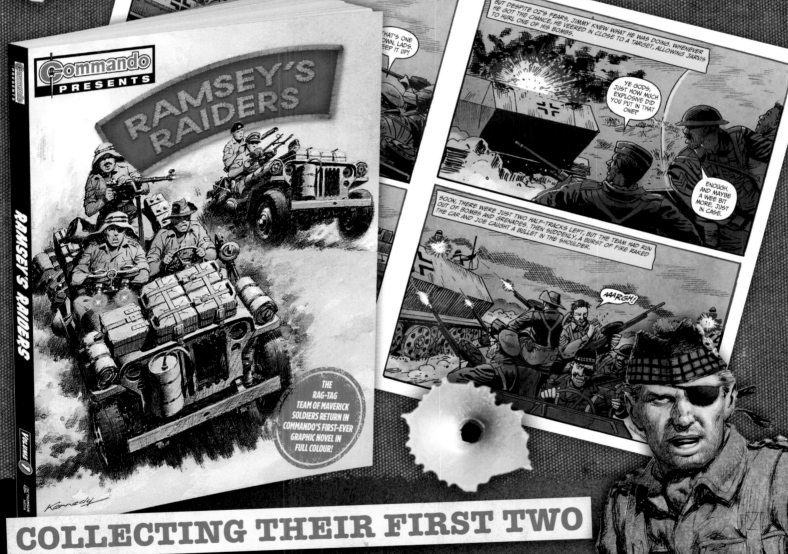